R is for Rhode Island Red

A Rhode Island Alphabet

Written by Mark R. Allio and Illustrated by Mary Jane Begin

We'd like to thank all of the willing participants who kindly posed for pictures and those who encouraged us every step of the way. Thank you Mom, Dad, Gates, Liam, Robert and Barbara Allio, Camillo Eifler, John Mott, Bob Paolo, Katie Dubois, Danny and the Begin family, the Waterman, Scorza and Stamatakos families, and all of the friends and neighbors who contributed great ideas!

We'd also like to thank all of the companies and institutions that gave permission or who provided vital information that helped in the creation of this book. Thank you to the Pawtucket Red Sox, the Rhode Island Historical Society, Bill Mulholland of Rhode Island Parks and Recreation, Slater Park Carousel, Modern Diner, Del's Frozen Lemonade, Stephan Goldman of New England Pest Control, the Rhode Island Tourism and Visitor Bureau, Ed Lane and Wayne Charness of Hasbro, Slater Mill Museum and the Providence Art Club, the Astor's Beechwood Mansion, Save the Bay, Rhode Island Red Society, Roger Williams Society, Costantino's Venda Ravioli, and the City of Providence.

Sleeping Bear Press™

310 North Main Street, Suite 300
Chelsea, MI 48118
www.sleepingbearpress.com

THOMSON
★
GALE

© 2005 Thomson Gale, a part of the Thomson Corporation.

Thomson, Star Logo and Sleeping Bear Press are trademarks and Gale is a registered trademark used herein under license.

Printed and bound in China.

10 9 8 7 6 5 4 3 2

Library of Congress Cataloging-in-Publication Data

Allio, Mark R.
R is for Rhode Island Red : a Rhode Island alphabet / written by Mark R. Allio; illustrated by Mary Jane Begin.
p. cm.
ISBN 1-58536-149-6
1. Rhode Island—Juvenile literature. 2. English language—Alphabet—Juvenile literature. I. Begin, Mary Jane, ill. II. Title.
F79.3.A44 2005
974.5—dc22   2005005886

To my mother and father, who made me an Independent Man,
to Gates and Liam, through their young eyes I see again
and to Mary Jane, with whom I have truly found Providence.

MARK

❧

To my Aunt Annette,
known to many as Sister Jacqueline Marie,
for her wit, wisdom, tenacious spirit,
and life long dedication to teaching.

MARY JANE

A a

A is for Apple.

Whether you try it in a pie
or take it off the tree,
our state chose the Greening.
One bite and you'll agree!

Spelling books always pair a letter with a word, and **A** is usually for Apple. So we thought we'd begin your journey through Rhode Island with the state fruit, the Rhode Island Greening Apple! When William Blaxton moved to Rhode Island and planted his orchard in 1635, in keeping with farming tradition, he got to name the first apple grown in an orchard in America! He named his apple Blaxton's Yellow Sweeting but somehow the name was changed to Sweet Rhode Island Greening.

This medium-size apple has a green skin that becomes more yellow when ripening on the tree. Its juicy, tart fruit is delicious eaten raw, and its taste and texture make it perfect for apple pies. The Rhode Island Greening is now grown throughout the eastern and central United States from October to April. Do you like applesauce? Chances are that it was made from the Rhode Island Greening!

Native Americans lived in Rhode Island long before the arrival of Europeans. Historians believe its coastline was visited by the Irish, the Vikings, and the Portuguese, but it was the Italian explorer Giovanni da Verrazano who made the first "official" voyage in 1524. As Verrazano sailed through these waters, he saw an island 12 miles off-shore and wrote in his log that it looked like the Greek island of Rhodes, which many believe was the beginning of the state's name.

Almost a century later, in 1614, Dutch mariner Adriaen Block also sailed through these waters and came ashore to the island, which he named "Block Island" (after himself!) The island is only six miles long by three miles wide, but its towering seaside bluffs, rolling hills, and 365 freshwater ponds (one for each day of the year), make it a local treasure, named by the Nature Conservancy as "one of the 12 last great places in the Western Hemisphere."

B is for Block Island.

Block Island, Rhode Island, a beautiful place to be,
    there in the distance towards the heart of the sea.
From its majestic bluffs to its peaceful shore,
    one visit there and you'll wish for more!

C is for Carousel.

I hear the music and sounds of children
laughing in delight.
I smell the popcorn and cotton candy
and see a thrilling sight!

Have you ever ridden a merry-go-round? Rhode Island has three of the nation's finest 150 remaining original hand-carved wooden carousels. The Flying Horse Carousel, located in Westerly, is the oldest operating carousel in America, built in the 1850s. Its horses hang by chains and so the faster it spins, the farther out the horses fly!

The Crescent Park Carousel, located in East Providence, was built in 1895 by Charles I.D. Looff, a Danish immigrant famous for his craftsmanship. Its 66 hand-carved figures include dragons, serpents, and 56 jumping horses, with no two alike.

The Slater Memorial Park Carousel, located in Pawtucket, is another antique Looff carousel built in the 1880s, said to be the fastest Looff carousel ever made. Hold on to your hat as you try to grab the brass ring!

Yes, it's true, diners started right here in Rhode Island. It was 1858 when 17-year-old Walter Scott decided to make more money by selling coffee and sandwiches from a basket to newspaper night workers in Providence. By 1872 business was booming, and Scott began to sell his food from a horse-drawn covered wagon parked outside the *Providence Journal* newspaper office. As word of his success spread, others began to offer food from larger and more elaborate wagons, which began to look like the dining cars on railroad trains. The word "diner" is said to be short for "railroad dining car" because some owners actually made their restaurants from old railroad passenger cars and trolleys. Some of the more famous include the Modern Diner in Pawtucket, the first diner to be listed on the National Register of Historic Places, and the Haven Brothers diner in Providence, which parks itself every summer and fall, as it has for the past 100 years, in front of City Hall.

D d

D is for Diner.

They began here in our state.
Most have neon light,
　　serving up home cooking
morning, noon, and night.

E e

E is for East Side.

Between the Moshassuck and the Seekonk
behold the famed East Side—
from College Hill to Fox Point,
a source of local pride.

The "East Side" is a famous Providence neighborhood known throughout the state for its history, buildings, and people. It was right here on the east side of the Moshassuck River where Roger Williams established the settlement that became the state capital. The East Side includes the largest single collection of National Historic Society buildings in America, with many located on or near Benefit Street, which has been called the "Mile of History." In the mid-1900s, when many of these old buildings were in danger of being torn down, one woman, Antoinette Downing, led an effort to save them, beginning a preservation movement across America. She became best known for her defense of the College Hill neighborhood in Providence, home to Benefit Street. Many of the restored grand mansions in Newport were also saved by Downing and her supporters, many of whom were women.

Like New York's Little Italy and Boston's North End, Providence has its own Italian neighborhood known as Federal Hill, located on the West side of the city. In 1788 Amos Maine Atwells led the development of the West Side, and the main street bears his name. During the first half of the nineteenth century, many Irish tradesmen, such as painters, carpenters, blacksmiths, cobblers, and longshoremen settled in this area. Then in the early 1900s more immigrants came, mainly from Italy, and soon it became one of the largest Italian settlements in the country. Although the neighborhood today has fewer people than it did originally, it still retains its historic character and Italian flavor. You can stop at one of the many cafes and bakeries, and help yourself to homemade pasta, pizza, an Italian ice, or a sweet cannoli. Mmmm, that's Italian!

F is for Federal Hill.

From Naples and from Tuscany,
from Sicily and Rome—
The old West Side of Providence
is where they made their home.

F f

Gg

On June 10th, 1772 an event took place here that set the stage for America's quest for independence—the burning of the ship *Gaspee*. In the 1760s the English sent ships to harass merchant ships in local waters and collect more taxes. But Rhode Islanders had had enough. When the English ship *Gaspee* tried to stop the American ship *Hannah*, the *Hannah*'s captain lured the *Gaspee* onto a sandbar where she ran aground. Upon arriving in Providence, the *Hannah*'s captain reported the incident to local residents. That night, timing the tides and moonlight perfectly, a small band of patriots rowed their longboats to the stranded ship, where they took the crew prisoner and set fire to the ship near dawn. The English never caught those patriots responsible, and as news spread, other colonies were inspired to join the resistance, resulting in the Boston Tea Party (1773), "The Shot Heard 'Round the World" at Lexington (1775), and ultimately in the Declaration of Independence (1776).

G is for *Gaspee*.

The tide is right for us to fight.
The *Gaspee* won't let us be.
Let's take a trip and sink that ship
and set our people free!

H is for Hasbro.

All these games are fun to play.
OK now, roll the dice!
Hasbro makes the coolest games.
Sorry, you rolled twice!

In 1923 Henry and Helal Hassenfeld started a company in Providence called Hassenfeld Brothers that first sold textile products, then began manufacturing pencil boxes and school supplies. In the years since, the company now known as Hasbro (based in Pawtucket) has grown into one of the largest toy and game companies in the world. Along the way, Hasbro has introduced many of the world's best and most well-known toys and games, including Monoply (the world's best-selling board game), Scrabble, Mr. POTATO HEAD (the first toy ever advertised on TV), PLAY-DOH (its formula is still top secret!), the EASY-BAKE Oven, G.I. Joe (the world's first "action figure"), My Little Pony, Twister (kids love it—grownups too!), Transformers (robots in disguise), Furby (one of the best-selling toys of all time), and Beyblades. Hasbro has also worked to help children and families in need all over the world through its charitable foundations and the Hasbro Children's Hospital based right here in Rhode Island.

I is for Independent Man.

Look up and see Independent Man
standing way up high,
watching over all Rhode Island
with clear and trusty eye.

Look up at the top of the State House in Providence, and you will see the statue known as the Independent Man, representing freedom, independence, and personal liberty. Created by artist George Brewster in 1899, the statue was originally named "Hope," the state's motto, taken when founding father Roger Williams said to early settlers "Hope in the Divine." Standing more than 11 feet tall and weighing more than 500 pounds, the Independent Man was cast in bronze, but is covered in gold. He holds a 14-foot spear in his right hand and an anchor, the state symbol, rests at his feet. The anchor is said to represent hope and remind us of water, so important to our state. Standing more than 278 feet above Providence, the Independent Man has weathered blistering sun, blizzards, hurricanes, and has been struck by lightning 27 times, but maintains his watch over all Rhode Islanders.

I i

Starting with the nation's first yarn spinning mill, our state led the way for America's Industrial Revolution. Although Rhode Island became known for woolen goods, machine tools, foundries, and steam engines, its precious metals industry was so successful that the state was called the Jewelry Capital of the World, a title still claimed today. It all started in 1824 when Providence jewelers Nehemiah and Seril Dodge discovered a way to make inexpensive jewelry by putting a thin coating or "plating" of silver or gold on cheap metal. The goods made this way were called "costume jewelry" and became popular all over the world. At about the same time, jeweler and silversmith Jabez Gorham started the company that would become the nation's largest producer of silverware. This company also became famous for its statues and memorials like the Independent Man. Today Rhode Island is home to more than 1,000 companies who make jewelry, crystal, fine pens, trophies, medals, and awards sold worldwide.

J j

J is for Jewelry.
This beautiful jewelry must cost a lot. Thanks to Rhode Island— probably not!

K k

Our people were scattered to the winds.
The few that remain stay strong,
teaching others about our past
so that all can sing our song.

Long before colonists arrived, Rhode Island was inhabited by native people whose ancestors lived here thousands of years ago. The largest local tribes were the Wampanoags and the Narragansetts. When the English settled at Plymouth in 1620, it was the Wampanoags and their chief Massasoit who were friendly to the colonists. As more Europeans came, the Native Americans suffered through war, disease, and the seizing of their lands. Massasoit was succeeded in 1662 by his son, Metacom, known to the English as King Philip. In 1675 King Philip convinced all of the local tribes to band together to try to drive the white man from Indian lands, thus beginning a nearly two-year war. By late 1676 the Wampanoags and Narragansetts were almost wiped out, and remaining tribal members were forced to live on small reservations. Today, despite more than 325 years of hardship, these tribes' descendants continue their struggle to keep their traditions and culture alive.

L **l**

L is for Ida Lewis and Lighthouse.

Ida Lewis was skillful and brave,
saved so many from a watery grave.
Some said only men could be so strong.
Twenty-five rescues proved them all wrong.

With 400 miles of coastline and unpredictable New England weather, lighthouses were a necessity in Rhode Island. They were usually built of stone on remote shorelines to help sailors navigate their ships in fog and storms. The lighthouse "keepers" who lived in these outposts often risked their lives to help those needing rescue. Keepers were traditionally men, but one of the most famous keepers of all time was a woman, Ida Lewis. Born in Newport in 1842, Ida took over her father's duties at the Lime Rock lighthouse after he fell ill when she was just 17 years old. She became very skillful in handling a boat and was considered by some to be the best swimmer in Newport. After making many rescues single-handedly, the Society of the American Cross of Honor proclaimed her "The Bravest Woman in America." In 1879 the government finally designated Ida the official keeper of Lime Rock Light Station. A lighthouse keeper for her entire life, she died in 1911 while on duty, a great heroine to the end.

The seaside city of Newport was one of Rhode Island's first settlements. Sitting at the mouth of Narragansett Bay where it meets the Atlantic Ocean, it became a major seaport and played a key role in the state's maritime history. Although trade slowed during Revolutionary times, "The City by the Sea" became extremely popular in the 1800s. Wealthy industrialists and landowners came to enjoy its beauty during the summer months, and many built huge mansions and villas that served as their summer "cottages." These wealthy people became known as the "the 400," an elite group of the very rich, which included famous families like the Astors and the Vanderbilts. As the city grew in popularity, well-to-do families came to go sailing, fox hunting, and play polo, golf, and tennis. The most extravagant of the summer homes, such as the Astors' Beechwood Mansion, were built along Bellevue Avenue and Ocean Drive near the famous Cliff Walk, where they can still be seen today.

m
M

M is for Mansions.

It was the golden age of elegance,
opulence for all to see—
kings and queens and their castles
in the City-by-the-Sea.

N is for Narragansett.

Jumping into the briny water
many fish abound:
bass and dogfish and funny flounder.
Any sharks around?

Rhode Island's greatest geographical feature and natural resource is Narragansett Bay. Named after a local Native American tribe, the bay is an estuary, a place where freshwater from the land and rivers mixes with salt water from the sea. Estuaries are considered the most biologically productive ecosystems on earth. Narragansett Bay is home to over 40,000 species of life including fish, birds, lobster, clams, eelgrass, and even harbor seals. Created by melting glaciers over 5,000 years ago, the Bay holds 706 billion gallons of water! Narragansett Bay has served as a source of food, commerce, and play for millions of people since colonial times, but its ecology has suffered. Pollution has reduced or eliminated some of the plant and wildlife species that once lived there. Happily, during the past 40 years concerned citizens, government agencies, local universities, and organizations like Save The Bay have worked hard to make people more aware of this fragile ecosystem, and make sure that it is used wisely by all.

N n

Rhode Island is the smallest of the 50 states, but it has the longest official name, which is the "State of Rhode Island and Providence Plantations." "Rhode Island" originally referred to Aquidneck Island where Newport, Middletown, and Portsmouth were located. "Providence Plantations" referred to the mainland portion of the state which was originally all part of Providence. Sound confusing? Many people thought so, and in searching for an easier nickname, came up with "The Ocean State," which you will see on every license plate. This name makes a lot of sense in a state that has 400 miles of coastline, 35 islands, and water covering more than 10% of its total area. Our fishing, shipbuilding, and maritime trade heritage is reflected in the state flag, which has an anchor in its center circled by 13 yellow stars representing the 13 original colonies. A blue ribbon under the anchor is emblazoned with the word "HOPE," our state motto, the shortest of all 50 states!

O is for Ocean State.

One thing can be said for sure
as you look around—
All throughout the Ocean State
water can be found.

P is for Providence.

Born of a vision for a perfect land
where people would be free.
Is Providence real or just a dream?
You'll have to come and see!

Pp

In 1636 Roger Williams established a new colony here which he named "Providence" in gratitude for "God's merciful providence." It was founded on the principles of personal and religious freedom, separation of church and state, and fair and equitable treatment of all people. Providence has suffered through the King Philip's War, economic downturns, even hurricanes, but the city has endured. Today Providence is the capital and largest city in Rhode Island and the third largest in New England, home to Brown University, Providence College, the Rhode Island School of Design (RISD), and Johnson and Wales University. In recent years, the downtown has been revitalized, and Providence is now called the "Renaissance City" a name evoking a golden age in Italy. Arts and cultural happenings abound, such as Waterfire, a frequent warmer weather event where sweet-smelling bonfires are lit atop the river at dusk, and people stroll the riverside while marveling at street performers, unusual music, and Italian gondolas that slip through the water.

If there is one thing that Rhode Islanders love, it would be the clam known as the quahog, special enough to have been named the official state "animal." Though some pronounce it KWO-hog, and others KWA-hog, most Rhode Islanders say KO-hog, a short-ened version of the Narragansett Indian word "poquauhock." Scientists named it for the Latin word meaning "wages," because local Indians used quahog shells to make wampum (beads that were used as money). Since quahogs prefer less salty water, estuaries like Narragansett Bay make a perfect home. Quahogs live buried just below the water's surface in the bottom sand or mud. You can figure out a quahog's age by counting the growth rings on its shell. Some large quahogs that are four inches or more long can be as much as 40 years old! And if you are really lucky, you might just find one that holds a rare purple pearl!

Qq

Q is for Quahog.

As the tide went out I stopped in the sand.
I dug on down and pulled out with my hand,
one clam, two clam, three clam, four.
Enough for a stuffie and a little bit more!

R r

It is said that 100 years ago at a New Bedford market, a sailor gave William Tripp of Little Compton, Rhode Island a red chicken that supposedly came from Malay in the Far East. Tripp took it back to his farm and began crossbreeding it with other types of birds. The final breed, which became known as a "Tripp fowl," was a handsome reddish bird that produced many eggs and had plenty of meat for a tasty meal. Little Compton soon became the most famous poultry town in America. Other local farmers began breeding their own versions of the famed bird, including Isaac Wilbour, whose farm became the largest in the country. When two local college professors decided that the birds were special enough to become a new breed, they asked Farmer Wilbour what he wanted to name his birds. He replied, "Why wouldn't Rhode Island Reds do?" and the rest is history. The Red was designated an official breed in 1895 and became the state's official bird in 1954.

R is for Rhode Island Red.

The roosters have plenty of meat.
The hens will lay eggs all year.
Known far and wide throughout the land,
Rhode Island Reds came from here.

Born in 1768, Samuel Slater has been called the Father of the American Industrial Revolution. As a young apprentice in England, he learned about textiles and the machinery used to make them. Coming to America in 1789, he built one of the first factories, or mills, in the United States in 1790 on the Blackstone River. This famous river was named after the Reverend William Blackstone, the first European to settle in Boston who then moved to Cumberland, Rhode Island. Three years later, Slater built Slater Mill in Pawtucket, the first American factory to spin cotton yarn using water-powered machines, launching the birth of the spinning industry. Industrialists flocked to the Blackstone River Valley hoping to copy Slater's methods and success, including his "Rhode Island System," where entire families worked in the mills and lived in villages created by the mill owners.

S s

By the early 1900s practically every town on the river had a mill, and the Blackstone was called "The hardest working river in America." Although many of these families came from Italy, Ireland, and Portugal, the majority came from the French-Canadian province of Quebec, with many settling in Woonsocket. Sadly, much of the success of these mills was due to child labor. Slater's first employees were all children from seven to twelve years old. Most worked long hours in unhealthy factories for less than $1 per week, and were not allowed to play or even go to school, except for the wealthy few. It was not until 1938 that child labor was finally eliminated with the passage of the Fair Labor Standards Act.

S is for Samuel Slater.

Slater Mill, that's where I am
working that machine,
spinning 15 hours or more.
Next year I turn thirteen.

Hungry? Rhode Island has treats that you won't find anywhere else. Coffee milk (milk mixed with coffee syrup) has been so popular for so long it's the official state drink. Add ice cream, and you have what is called a Cabinet, supposedly because its creator kept his blender in a "kitchen cabinet." Our "clam shacks" proudly serve up clam cakes, "stuffies," and clear chowder (all made with clams, of course). Many states have Italian ice stands in the cities, but here you can find Del's Frozen Lemonade served throughout the state even in winter. We do love our pizza strips (slices of crust with pizza sauce, no cheese, served unheated). Anyone can make a pancake, but here we have jonnycakes (griddle pancakes made from local white cap flint corn). Their name probably came from early settlers who stuffed them into pockets when traveling and called them "journey cakes."

Tt

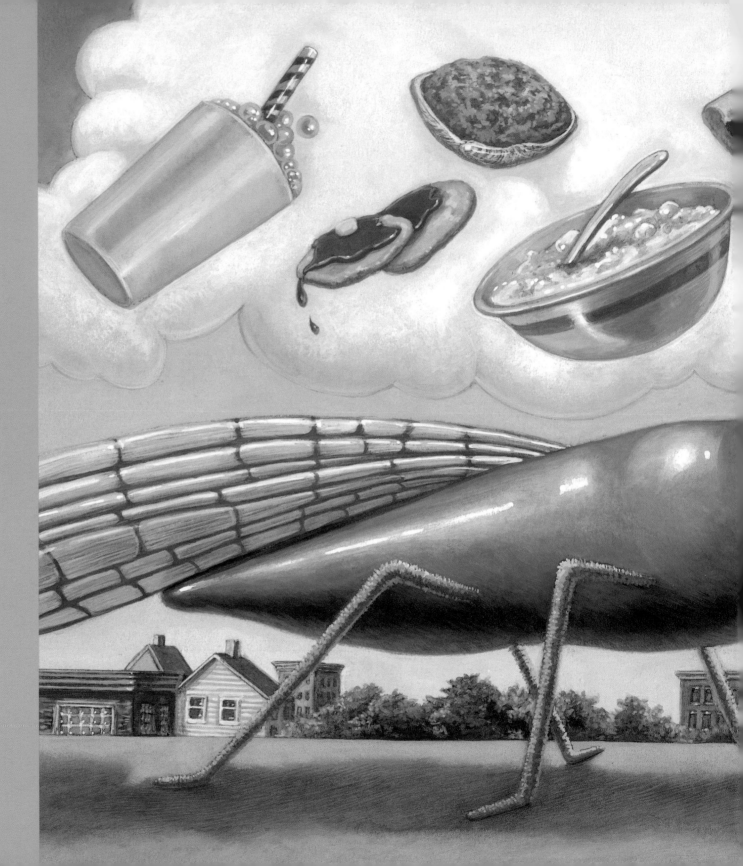

T is for Tasty Treats.

Noontime came and it was time for lunch.
Started me thinking about what I could munch.
I stopped at a diner to see what they had.
Hey those jonnycakes aren't looking too bad!

All right, we've all seen big bugs, but the one that takes the cake has got to be Nibbles. He's not a real live bug, but a model of a big blue termite on the roof of the New England Pest Control building on the highway just south of Providence. At 58 feet long (928 times actual termite size), "Nibbles Woodaway" is definitely the World's Largest Bug! The company likes to dress Nibbles up on holidays, and gives him an Uncle Sam hat on Independence Day, a witch's hat and broom on Halloween, and a red blinking nose and antlers on Christmas. Wave hello to Nibbles as you drive past. He is surely dreaming of all the tasty treats Rhode Island has to offer!

Although our state was always a haven for those escaping persecution, and the first state to pass a law banning slavery, much of its early wealth came from the Triangle Trade (the trading of rum, molasses, and slaves between Rhode Island, the West Indies, and Africa). In the years leading up to and through the Civil War, both Newport and Providence served as whistle stops on the so-called Underground Railroad. The Underground Railroad was not exactly a railroad, nor was it underground, but a secret way for runaway slaves to escape their masters in the South and find freedom in the North and Canada. Between 1830 and 1860, more than 50,000 slaves were given transportation and shelter in safe houses on the perilous journey northward. Famous Rhode Island havens included Newport's Touro Synagogue, the oldest Hebrew church in North America, and the African Freedmen's Society of Rhode Island, established in Providence by former slave Ichabod Northrup.

U u

U is for Underground Railroad.

It doesn't matter how you look.
We all deserve our pride.
    I wonder why more folks don't know
that we're all the same inside.

V V

V is for Violet.

Here you'll find violets and big red maples,
magnetic rocks, and ocean spray.
And spend long hours dreaming
about the bass that got away!

With its bay and ocean coast, low altitude and woodsy inland areas, nature abounds in Rhode Island. The state flower is the violet, a beautiful small purple flower that grows in woods, thickets, and limy areas. The state tree is the red maple, a medium-size tree found throughout the state. The state fish is the striped bass, a fisherman's favorite. It usually measures 20-30 inches long and weighs 3-10 pounds, but one lucky local fisherman caught one 55 inches long and weighing 70 pounds! Do you remember reading about our state fruit and state animal? Bowenite, the state mineral, is considered a semiprecious stone closely related to jade. Cumberlandite, the state rock, is a rare stone not found anywhere else in the world. A heavy black or dark brown rock with white markings, it will actually attract a magnet! Because of its pitted surface and magnetic content, it is often mistaken for a meteorite.

No one is more responsible for the creation of Rhode Island than Roger Williams, who in his search for freedom founded what became the first democratic state of modern times. Born about 1603, he chose to become a minister in the Church of England. As a young clergyman, he embraced Puritanism, a new way of thinking in the church, and agreed to bring this philosophy to colonies in the New World. Arriving in Boston in 1631, he was first welcomed, but then the local Puritans disapproved of his views that the king had no right to give away lands belonging to the Indians, that everyone was entitled to their own opinion regarding religion, and that church and state should be separate. In 1636, when the local authorities decided to send Williams back to England, he fled southwest, bought land from his Indian friends, and established the settlement of Providence.

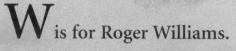

W is for Roger Williams.

Roger Williams had a vision so clear.
Crossed over from England to make it known here.
His ideas the Puritans could not understand
so he came to Rhode Island to found a new land.

His colony became a haven for Quakers, Jews, and others fleeing from religious persecution, including Anne Hutchinson, who became the first woman to establish her own settlement in America (in Portsmouth). As more and more Europeans came to the area, Williams often acted as a peacemaker between the colonists and the Indians. Although Williams died in 1683, his name graces a number of institutions throughout the state, including a university, a park and zoo, and a national memorial devoted to this profound thinker. There is no known painting made of him during his lifetime, but his ideas, words, and deeds live on.

From 1650 to 1700, as the number of merchant ships grew, many captains obtained official commissions as "privateers," allowing them to legally capture ships for the king and keep a portion of the booty. When some of these privateers struck out on their own, plundering ships and taking all the booty for themselves, they became known as pirates. As more locals signed up to be pirate crew members, Rhode Island began to develop a reputation as a pirate refuge. Some of the more famous pirates known to have spent time here include Long Ben, Blackbeard, Captain Kidd, and Rhode Island's very own Thomas Tew the Pirate. Born to a wealthy Newport family, Tew grew up to be a skilled captain and privateer.

X
x

X marks the spot.

Thomas Tew the Pirate
some say he did but good.
Took from others what we wanted
a high seas Robin Hood!

While sailing his ship to Africa on a difficult mission with small reward, Tew decided instead to capture ships carrying vast riches that were crossing the Persian Gulf and the Red Sea. He asked his crew, who supposedly vowed, "A gold chain or a wooden leg, we'll stand by you," and they crossed the line into piracy. In 1694 Tew returned to Newport fabulously wealthy from plundering these cargo ships. The townspeople welcomed him as a hero, and as his success became known throughout the colonies, he was called the "Robin Hood of the Red Sea." Six months later, he decided to do it again, but met his end while trying to take another ship. Even though Tew was not considered a pirate at home, his exploits inspired legions of new pirates and began what some call the golden age of piracy

Yy

Y is for Yachting.

Ahoy there, matey, what do you say?
Won't you come aboard our ship?
Built for speed out of Bristol town,
she will sail at one brisk clip!

A yacht (pronounced "yot") is a smaller sailing or motor-powered boat used for pleasure cruising or racing. Boats have always been a part of Rhode Island history, and we have led the way in designing and building world-class boats for work and for play. Have you heard about the America's Cup, the oldest and most famous sailboat race in the world? For more than 150 years, sailors from around the globe have competed every four years for the honor of winning the trophy cup. For an unbroken stretch of 132 years (1851 to 1983), the United States won the race, often using legendary boats designed and built by Rhode Islanders. One boat builder, Captain Nathaniel G. Herreshoff, was a Rhode Islander thought by many to be the greatest marine designer and builder this country has ever produced. Today the area known as the East Bay (including Newport, Portsmouth, Bristol, and Warren) remains one of the largest boat-building centers in the country.

Z is for Zephyr.

You can search the whole country
North, South, East, and West.
But nowhere is a place like this.
Little Rhody, you're the best!

The word zephyr (pronounced "zeffer") is used to describe a westerly wind or gentle breeze. In Rhode Island, the wind almost always blows from the west, and we actually have a town called Westerly, located on the state's southwestern tip. A frontier town of the new colony, Westerly's Indian name was Misquamicut (a place for taking salmon), a name still used today for one of the town's beautiful beaches. In days past, the town supplied granite rock used for buildings and monuments throughout the country, but it is best known now as a vacation destination. Families flock to see its beautiful rock formations and sand beaches, its wonderful views of the ocean, and attractions like Watch Hill with its famous carousel. As you feel the breeze, and see the people swimming, sailing, fishing, or just enjoying life, you will know why Rhode Islanders believe that "The Ocean State" is one of the most beautiful places on earth!

A Quahog Full of Questions

1. Who gave Rhode Island its name—Verrazano, Adriaen Block, or Roger Williams?

2. What form of government does the United States have, and what are some of its important principles?

3. What is the name of the statue that sits on top of the Rhode Island State House?

4. Who is called the Father of the American Industrial Revolution?

5. What was the name of the ship that Rhode Island patriots burned which ultimately led to the Revolutionary War and independence from England?

6. What is "costume" jewelry?

7. Who was King Philip?

8. What original Rhode Island settlement was called the "City by the Sea"?

9. Name three things that you can find in Narragansett Bay.

10. What is a quahog?

11. What is the capital of Rhode Island and what does its name mean?

12. What is Rhode Island's state bird?

13. What was the Underground Railroad?

14. What's so special about Cumberlandite, Rhode Island's state rock?

15. Who was Roger Williams and why was he a great man?

16. Which of the following pirates came from Rhode Island—Blackbeard, Thomas Tew, or Captain Kidd?

17. What is the America's Cup?

18. What is a yacht?

19. Rhode Island has the shortest motto of all the states. What is it?

20. What symbol is on the Rhode Island state flag and seal?

Answers

1. All three.

2. Democracy. Separation of church and state, freedom of choice, all people are equal.

3. The Independent Man.

4. Samuel Slater, inventor of the first water-powered spinning yarn machine.

5. The *Gaspee*.

6. Jewelry that is "plated" with a thin coating of silver or gold instead of solid.

7. He was the Wampanoag Indian chief that led an uprising of New England Indian tribes against the colonists to try to take back tribal lands.

8. Newport.

9. Clams, fish, lobsters, birds, eelgrass, seals.

10. A hard shell clam.

11. Providence. A place that is under divine care.

12. The Rhode Island Red.

13. The name given to the secret journey made by thousands of slaves looking for freedom in the North and Canada.

14. It is magnetic and it is only found in Rhode Island.

15. The founder of Rhode Island and a great thinker whose ideas gave birth to American democracy.

16. Thomas Tew, the Pirate from Newport.

17. The oldest international sailing race in the world.

18. A smaller sailing or motor-powered boat used for pleasure cruising or racing.

19. Hope.

20. An anchor.

Mary Jane Begin

Mary Jane Begin's illustration career began as a student at the Rhode Island School of Design, where she now teaches. Her award-winning picture book portfolio includes *Before I Go To Sleep, A Mouse Told His Mother, The Porcupine Mouse, Little Mouse's Painting, Wind in the Willows,* and *The Sorcerer's Apprentice.* She is the recipient of numerous awards including Awards of Excellence from *Communication Arts* and The Society of Illustrators as well as the Critici Erba Prize from the Bologna Book Fair. Mary Jane has provided book-making workshops and presentations to elementary schools across the country and maintains a website at: www.maryjanebegin.com.

Mark R. Allio

From the first time he went to Block Island as a teen, Mark Allio fell in love with Rhode Island. After years of visiting, he got his chance to live here in 1995, and has been happy as a clam ever since. He proposed to his wife, Mary Jane, atop Block Island's Mohegan Bluffs, and they now live with their two children and yellow lab in Barrington within view of Narragansett Bay. Holding degrees in liberal arts and business, Mark has worked as an arts administrator, consultant, and entrepreneur. His interests include music, exploration, and the martial arts. This book is his first published work.